Who Lives in a Tree?

Susan Canizares • Daniel Moreton

SCHOLASTIC INC.

Acknowledgments

Science Consultants: Patrick R. Thomas, Ph.D., Bronx Zoo/Wildlife Conservation Park; Glenn Phillips, The New York Botanical Garden; **Literacy Specialist:** Maria Utefsky, Reading Recovery Coordinator, District 2, New York City

Design: MKR Design, Inc.

Endnotes: Susan Russell

Credits

Photos ©: cover: stock_shot/Shutterstock; 1: TongRo Images Inc/Thinkstock; 2: Daniel J Cox/Getty Images; 3: epantha/iStockphoto; 4: Gytis/Thinkstock; 5: Eric Gevaert/Shutterstock; 6: Maurizio Bonora/iStockphoto; 7: Bruce Macqueen/Dreamstime; 8: stock_shot/Shutterstock; 9: zorandimzr/iStockphoto; 10: visionsofmaine/iStockphoto; 11: JHaviv/Thinkstock; 12: Mary Plage/Getty Images; 13 top left: Daniel J Cox/Getty Images; 13 top right: epantha/iStockphoto; 14 top right: Bruce Macqueen/Dreamstime; 14 center left: stock_shot/Shutterstock; 14 center right: zorandimzr/iStockphoto; 14 bottom left: visionsofmaine/iStockphoto; 14 bottom right: JHaviv/Thinkstock.

Copyright © 2012, 1998 by Scholastic Inc.
All rights reserved. Published by Scholastic Inc.
Printed in the U.S.A.

ISBN-13: 978-0-545-54940-0
ISBN-10: 0-545-54940-X

17 18 19 20 21   132   27 26 25 24 23 22

Scholastic Inc., 557 Broadway, New York, NY 10012

Who lives in a tree?

Raccoons live in trees.

Butterflies live in trees.

Foxes live in trees.

Ladybugs live in trees.

Woodpeckers live in trees.

Squirrels live in trees.

Chipmunks live in trees.

Hedgehogs live in trees.

Porcupines live in trees.

Owls live in trees.

Bats live in trees—upside down!

Who Lives in a Tree?

Trees are full of good things for people. They give us shade for keeping cool, paper for writing, medicines to help us get well when we are sick, wood to build our houses, fruits and nuts to eat, and much more. And for some members of the animal kingdom, trees can provide the most important things for living: food and shelter. Here are some of the animals and insects that rely on trees..

Baby raccoons (left) are playing inside the papery bark of a birch tree. These playful animals find shelter in hollow logs and love to eat the fruit that trees provide. The monarch butterflies (right) migrate thousands of miles each year to return to the very same trees deep in Mexico and Central America. It is still a mystery how this happens!

Two baby foxes look out from their den which their mother made out of the bottom of a tree trunk. The mother fox depends on the tree to keep her babies safe while she goes out to hunt for food. The tiny ladybugs (right) that we are all familiar with are often found in large groups on tree branches. Here, they are feeding on the sap from a pine tree.

The woodpecker (left) uses hollow places in trees as a safe nest for its young. It also pecks holes in the bark that covers the tree to find insects to eat. The squirrel (right), who loves to eat nuts, builds its nest high in the branches of a tree. The nest is called a drey and is like a hollow ball, with leaves and twigs on the outside and soft grasses lining the inside.

The chipmunk (left) uses holes in tree trunks as warehouses for winter food. Chipmunks stuff their cheeks with nuts and seeds so they don't have to make as many trips back and forth. That way, they lessen their chances of meeting a predator. The hedgehog (right), who also favors a home in a hollow tree, rolls up in a ball when threatened, showing only its prickly spines.

The porcupine (left) is a good climber and will climb a tree if chased! But if an enemy gets close to the porcupine, it backs into its attacker, releasing long quills and piercing the attacker's skin. Owls (right) use the twigs that a tree provides to make a safe nest to raise their young. At night, the tree becomes a lookout post for nocturnal hunting raids.